Search Manual
for
Discovering and Using Your Spiritual Gifts

**A Neighborhood or Church
Spiritual Search
For Friendly People Reaching Out and Up**

Search and Leadership Format By
Gus Gustafson

Includes Leader's Guide

Contents

Introduction

Five-week Search Group
Exploration and Discovery
30 minutes daily for 30 days
produces power for accomplishment beyond your imagination!

"Glory to Him whose power, working in us,
can do infinitely more than we can ask or imagine."
Ephesians 3:20, *Jerusalem Bible*

This spiritual growth program consists of:
1. Bible (furnished by participant)

2. Scriptural study guides

   a. Booklet: *Discovering Your Spiritual Gifts*

   b. Guided lectures on cassette tapes

      (1) "An Introduction to Spiritual Gifts"

      (2) "Biblical Principles and Spiritual Gifts"

      (3) "Discovering Your Spiritual Gifts"

      (4) "Spiritual Gifts and The Church"

3. Format for personal, creative exploration

4. Leadership guide for Search Group Appraisal and Affirmation (within workbook)

This package generates powerful spiritual motivation by combining:

1. Bible study
2. Personal outreach to God
3. Appraisal and affirming guidance through group dynamics
4. Follow-up action

This will be a wonderful experience!
Discover your spiritual gifts.
Learn to use your spiritual gifts more effectively for lasting accomplishment to the glory of God.

Acknowledgments

God speaks and guides in many different and unexpected ways. Frequently for me, He works through people. So often the word I get from the Lord is affirmed and/or made clear through one or more of His faithful and dedicated servants. *Discovering and Using Your Spiritual Gifts* was developed through the influence of such people.

Discovering your spiritual gifts is one of the most exciting exercises in the 29-day "Discover God's Call" experience which is done simultaneously by people representing many local churches over a wide area. The climax of this venture is a weekend where the "explorers" meet in one place. The study places an emphasis on service, and participants determine the needs of their congregations. Then they match their gifts with the church's needs. So often I've heard ideas from these weekend "discoverers" such as, "I wish we could spend more time on the gifts," or "I'd like to have more people in our church know about the gifts."

One day Nancy Sampson of Asbury United Methodist Church in Greenville, Tennessee, asked, "Couldn't we develop a study on the spiritual gifts that we could use for small groups in our church?" I agreed.

After talking and praying with Ken Kinghorn, author of the key guide booklet, *Discovering Your Spiritual Gifts*, we decided I should develop the search and leadership format. Ken would review and make suggested approaches.

Charles Kinder and Ross Freeman furnished crucial leadership in starting the parent program, "Discover God's Call." As they encouraged us to move ahead with "Discover," they promised their support and guidance as new directions and needs arose. At the same time we stepped out in faith, not knowing just where the Lord would be leading. We started with Moses' prayer: "Guide me clearly along the road you want me to travel..." (Exodus 33:13, *The Living Bible*). Ken and I are deeply grateful for their review of and contribution to this study.

My wife, Estelle, is at the very heart of the entire "Discover God's Call" program. Without her input and hours of labor we very likely would not have finished this search guide.

I also think of Lynn Beckman, a young Christian mother and secretary who frequently stopped by to pick up the manuscript at 7 a.m. or earlier to keep the typing on schedule.

"No eye has seen, no ear has heard, no mind has conceived what God has prepared for those who love him" (1 Corinthians 2:9).

Gus Gustafson

A Word About the Word

This search exercise is written to be a dialogue between you and the Holy Spirit, with you listening predominantly to the Holy Spirit. The purpose of this study is not to promote the writers' ideas. Instead, we want you to give yourself to God for His direction through His Word and the Holy Spirit.

The writers' roles are to:

1. Bring to the surface portions of scripture that point the way to spiritual self-discovery.

2. Provide tested practices, revealed by God, for self-understanding.

3. Offer an effective way for communicating with the Holy Spirit.

4. Help you understand your gifts as related to the needs in your areas of influence.

5. Guide you to experience an exciting exploration and a life-empowering discovery!

If you approach this search with the open-minded attitude of determining God's will for your life, you will discover more than you can imagine.

"However, as it is written: 'No eye has seen, no ear has heard, no mind has conceived what God has prepared for those who love him...' " (1 Corinthians 2:9).

"Call to me and I will answer you and tell you great and unsearchable things you do not know" (Jeremiah 33:3).

This search is written with the conviction that no study guide is as powerful or as wise as the Holy Scriptures. You may use the translation of your choice. As the Word of God it will speak to you. Some translations are used for intensive study; some are used for devotional reading and to get a good overview of scripture. For our standard text we are using and recommending The New International Version. A good alternate is the *The Living Bible,* a modern paraphrase. Throughout the study we suggest you look up specific passages in translations other than the NIV. If you do not have access to those translations, just refer to the version of the Bible you regularly use.

Out of this self-giving study we expect to see inspired lay leadership emerge to help lead the spiritual renewal that is moving across our land.

May our good and great God richly bless you as you embark on a venture that will lead to a great discovery—your great potential and ability to respond to God's call for your life.

About the Author

Gus (M.O.) Gustafson is the author of *Called To Be A Layman, What's God Saying To Me?*, numerous study guides and free-lance articles. A retired businessman, he organized and is National Director of "Discover God's Call" for the Foundation For Evangelism of the United Methodist Church. He also developed the "Weekend for Winners." He and his wife, Estelle, spend considerable time coordinating the program in local churches.

Launching Your Exploration

A Pre-Search Party

This experience of *Discovering and Using Your Spiritual Gifts* will be a high venture of spirit and mind. Let us start with an exciting pre-search party!

It would be a good idea for someone to invite the group into his or her home for an evening. Others should bring refreshments. Allow one and one-half hours for this event. Plan on 30 minutes for refreshments and fellowship and one hour for organization and getting to know each other better.

Here's what you should do at the pre-search party:

1. If more than 12 people are participating, form two or more groups. This will greatly enrich the experience of all. This search and discovery experience is maximized in groups of six to twelve.

2. Designate the captain of each search group. This person is elected for the full time of the search. The captain makes sure that each session has a leader and a place to meet as well as taking care of other details to keep each group progressing.

Captain's name: ____ .

3. I recommend that the captain select a different leader for each of the five forthcoming search sessions. An alternative method is to have two or three people rotate leadership. Leadership is simplified by following "Tips For Search Group Leaders," found in the addendum, pages 75-76.

4. List names of leaders for each session on the first page of each Group Exploration and Celebration format at the end of each week's study.

5. List the homes where the different sessions will be held:

      Date   Home

1.

2.

3.

4.

5.

6. Pass out the search materials to each individual participating. Every person should have a search manual, the *Discovering Your Spiritual Gifts* booklet and the guided lectures on cassette tapes.

7. After taking care of the organizational considerations, discuss these two questions as an introduction to the search and to each other. Be as specific and personal as possible.

    1.What do I expect to get out of this group search?

    2. In what way can knowledge of my spiritual gifts make my life more effective?

8. Important: Get off to a positive start. Close the meeting right on time, or earlier!

9. Finally, form a bond of fellowship with everyone standing in a circle and holding hands if they feel comfortable doing so. One person should lead a short prayer. Then, everyone should recite the Lord's Prayer in unison.

Why Spiritual Gifts?

Week 1—Day 1

Introductory Information for Exploration

Your mind-opening sentence prayer for today's search:

Let my mind and spirit be open to the new things You are about to show me.

Discovering and using your spiritual gifts are:

Exciting

Most of us have an inborn curiosity about who we are, the characteristics that tell the world what we are, the abilities that can make us the most effective, the spiritual gifts through which supernatural power can flow. Many of us have vague ideas of these things but need confirmation and affirmation. This all makes the possibility of discovering our spiritual gifts very intriguing.

Two professional women, by discovering their spiritual gifts and offering them to God for His use, transformed a large metropolitan school system of more than 100 schools. These women, by giving themselves to God's call and confident of their spiritual gifts flowing through their lives, changed the school system's staff attitude of greed and grasping competition to one of service. That is exciting!

Energizing

When we discover our spiritual gifts—and let God use them—we become heirs to artesian-like wells of energy never before experienced.

One woman reported that after discovering her gifts she was able to accomplish things which previously she thought impossible. Her 60s and 70s turned out to be the most vibrant and vital years of her life.

Empowering

By becoming keenly aware of our spiritual gifts and offering them to Christ for His use through us, we receive *power* beyond our expectations or human reason. We experience confidence and courage that come from exercising our gifts within the harmony of God's will.

A retired man in his late 60s discovered that one of his top four gifts was giving. He prayed, "Lord, how can I give more, being retired and having no income other than social security and very modest investments?" The Lord gave him an idea. Within two years, his income was greater than it had been in any of his so-called productive, executive years. His giving more than doubled.

Through the use of our spiritual gifts God equips us with supernatural power!

Digging Directions

As you set out to mine the riches awaiting you, there are some logical guidelines that, followed faithfully, will lead you to your treasure. The outline will guide your five-week search.

1. "Why Spiritual Gifts?" Why should I search for them?

2. "Scriptural Identification of Spiritual Gifts." Names and how many.

3. "Function of Each Spiritual Gift." How should they be used?

4. "Discovering My Spiritual Gifts."

5. "Spiritual Gifts in Areas of Influence." How does God want to use my gifts?

Excavation Equipment

To unearth this priceless treasure, we are approaching our search with the following supernatural "excavation equipment" and methods. Using them makes this experience one of the greatest adventures in our lives.

Our resources include:

1. The Bible

2. Two-way prayer—petition and listening

3. Booklet—*Discovering Your Spiritual Gifts*

4. Guided lectures on cassette tapes—"The Gifts of The Spirit"

5. Workbook with discovery notes

6. Team appraisal and affirmation

Using these resources diligently will lead us to deep digging and to heavenly heights.

Disciplines For the Venture

The legendary coach of the Green Bay Packers football team, the late Vince Lombardi, had five disciplines for the Packers that lifted them from the cellar to the Super Bowl. Thomas Edison used carefully defined, intricate methods for checking phenomena resulting from experiments. From these disciplines he was able to spot significant facts that others missed, and he became an inventive genius.

So it is in this search. If you faithfully follow these seven search rules, you will capture a greater measure of the treasure and find greater satisfaction in the long run. Here are the guidelines:

1. Start each day's search with a written one or two sentence mind-and-heart-opening prayer. Note the sample for the first two days. Starting the third day, jot down your own prayer.

2. Turn to scripture for guidance. S. D. Gordon said you will know you are hearing the right voice by reading the Bible, ". . . as interpreted by the Spirit, and the Spirit as He speaks through His book" (*Quiet Talks on Power,* S. D. Gordon, Revell).

3. Do your search day by day. For the clearest understanding, do not (a) run ahead of the daily schedule or (b) condense two or more days into one sitting. In an emergency you may speed up or slow down the schedule, but do not mix it up. One exercise dovetails into the next. Do not listen to the tapes or read the booklet until they fit into your search.

4. Write down ideas that come to you as you listen, pray and search. There is a strong possibility that these ideas are from the Lord. Once you have written them down, you have

captured them! They become sub-discoveries leading to the big discovery for which you are searching.

5. You have one day a week to catch up, if necessary. You will notice this search uses only six days a week, leaving one for review or for pulling together loose ends.

6. Start your biblical exploration in the New International Version, a recent translation. Also use other versions you have. Cross-checking translations is a good way to develop a perceptive understanding of scripture for our day.

7. Finally, write in a summary sentence or two the new insights coming out of each day's search. This daily insight becomes an important step leading to your great discovery. (Use the bottom of the page at the end of each day's introduction.)

Vital Preparation For Our Venture

It will take discipline and persistence to appropriate fully your resources and reach your goal. So, how about doing these things to begin?

1. Write down the time of day you will be doing your explorations. You should plan to set aside thirty minutes daily.

    a.m. (or)

_______ p.m.
    Time

2. How are you going to find those thirty minutes? (Check one.)
( ) Get up earlier.*

( ) Stay up later.**

( ) Set aside time after getting your family off to work or school.

( ) Use the time already being used for Bible study, prayer or reading.

( ) Other:

*After your body has adjusted to the new time schedule (two or three days), the energy lost in 30 minutes of sleep will be replaced with inspired energy. It's hard to believe until it's experienced.

**If you are a night person, your personal exploration can become so moving that you will have a hard time going to sleep.

3. State below, in no more than two sentences, why you look forward to doing the search in *Discovering and Using Your Spiritual Gifts.*

4. This may be new to you, but try it. In not more than four sentences write the prayer of your heart as you approach this journey.

Your insight from today's search:

Week 1 — Day 2

The Unique Characteristics of Spiritual Gifts

Your mind-opening sentence prayer for today's search:

Help me understand what's so special about spiritual gifts

---

1. Check these passages in more than one version if you have them: 1 Corinthians 12:31, 1 Timothy 4:14-15 and 2 Timothy 1:6-7.

2. Words from the Lord (Write two or three sentences of what the scripture says to you.):

3. Your understanding of spiritual gifts

Mark **T** or **F** to the left of the statements below. Do not worry about the answers now. We will give you the answers in a week, after you have re-taken the quiz. You will be pleased by your new understanding.

True or False

Today date ________		*Next week* date ________
1. ( )	Love is a spiritual gift.	( )
2. ( )	Spiritual gifts are as important to lay people as to pastors.	( )
3. ( )	A spiritual gift gives us supernatural ability.	( )
4. ( )	Both Christians and non-Christians have spiritual gifts.	( )
5. ( )	I can identify my spiritual gifts.	( )
6. ( )	Spiritual gifts are God's instruments for channeling supernatural power through Christians.	( )
7. ( )	Talents may be spiritual gifts.	( )
8 ( )	Spiritual gifts are manifested only through people committed to Jesus Christ.	( )
9. ( )	Music is a spiritual gift.	( )
10. ( )	Knowledge of my spiritual gift can enhance its use.	( )
11. ( )	Patience is a spiritual gift.	( )
12. ( )	Spiritual gifts can be acquired through personal disciplines and study.	( )
13. ( )	I can develop my spiritual gifts.	( )

Your insight from today's search:

Week 1 — Day 3

Perspective on Spiritual Gifts

Your mind-opening sentence prayer for today's search:

---

1. Scriptural mind-opener: 1 Corinthians 12:4-7.

2. In no more than two sentences, write what these verses say to you.

3. Listen to the tape titled "An Introduction to Spiritual Gifts."

You will reap the fruit of hours of tedious and systematic biblical research on the gifts of the Spirit if you outline the tape as you listen to it. It will be easy to outline. Start here and continue on the next page.

Continue your outline here:

____

Your insight from today's search

____

Week 1 — Day 4

Spiritual Gifts and You

Your mind-opening sentence prayer for today's search:

---

1. Divine words of encouragement: Romans 12:6-8.

2. What do these verses say to you? Try summarizing them in two sentences or more. These are foundational scriptures for future study.

3. To uncover insights on spiritual gifts, read pages 7-9 in *Discovering Your Spiritual Gifts.*

4. Reflecting on what you have read, which of the ideas presented on pages 7-9 was the most significant to you? Or potentially, which one has the greatest meaning for your career and pastime activities? You be the judge. If you have difficulty selecting one, it is all right to list several below, but try to single out one.

Your insight from today's search:

Week 1 — Day 5

Spiritual Gifts and the Church

Your mind-opening sentence prayer for today's search:

---

1. Today's scriptural insight: 1 Peter 4:10-11.

2. What application do you see in these verses regarding the relationship between you and your church? Reread the scripture, inviting the Holy Spirit to speak to you. Write what you "hear."

3. Listen to the tape, "Biblical Principles and Spiritual Gifts." You will receive more insights on spiritual gifts, you and your church. Outline the message in the space provided.

Continue your outline here:

____

Your insight from today's search:

____

Week 1 — Day 6

The Great Importance of Spiritual Gifts

Your mind-opening sentence prayer for today's search:

---

1. Listen again to Paul's words about the great importance of spiritual gifts in the lives of Christians: 1 Corinthians 12:4-7.

2. Paul outlines several principles of kingdom-building in this scripture. Name three or more principles that come alive as you hear Paul speaking about how God's Church will grow.

3. Listen to the questions at the beginning of tape number three, "Discovering Your Spiritual Gifts."

4. Go back to Day 2 and check your current understanding of spiritual gifts by filling in the blanks on the right-hand side of the true-false questions.

5. After redoing your true-false exercise, check your answers in the addendum, p. 73.

6. Turn to the next page, "Group Exploration and Celebration," and write in your "mind-opening sentence prayer" to be used in your group meeting.

Your insight from today's search:

Week 1

Group Exploration and Celebration

Your mind-opening sentence prayer for today's exploration and celebration:

Name of leader ____

A. Preparation directions for the leader:

1. Read addendum, pages 75-76, "Tips for Search Group Leaders."

2. Make sure everyone has filled in "your mind-opening prayer." If not, take time for everyone to fill it in.

B. Bringing People's Hearts Together (30 minutes)

1. 20 minutes—Let informality and spontaneity be the atmosphere in which you bring your group together. First have every person share one good thing that has happened to him/her in the past week. Next let each person share personal news, joy and concerns, particularly centering on family, vocation, church and community. Include requests for prayer and prayers of thanksgiving for specific good things happening in the lives of group members.

2. 10 minutes—(a) Let each person read his/her mind-opening prayer for today's group experience with a prayerful attitude. (b) Stand in a circle to form a bond of fellowship with everyone holding hands if group members feel comfortable doing so. Ask each person to pray silently for the person on his/her right. Upon completion of each silent prayer, have every person squeeze the hand of the individual on his/her right. Next, repeat the process by asking all to pray silently for the person on their left. (c) Finally, open the floor for verbal sentence prayers from those who feel comfortable praying aloud. Suggest a special emphasis on praise for the ability to come together and petition for the presence and leading of the Holy Spirit. As the leader, you should conclude these brief prayers.

C. Exploration and Affirmation

In a relaxed fashion and a spirit of full acceptance of each others' ideas, raise these thoughts for sharing and discussion:

1. "Share-for-all" question: What single new idea from this week's study meant the most to you? Why? (Everyone should share one idea.)

2. Ask if anyone had difficulties (don't understand, don't agree with, can't make sense of) with points covered the past week. (Ask for a show of hands.) Then invite individuals to share any unresolved questions. After each question let the group respond. As leader, guide the responses to positive solutions. Guard against getting hung up on negatives. Instead, encourage upbeat thinking and lead that positive thinking to constructive answers.

3. Ask: How do spiritual gifts enrich your life? (Leader, bring out expressions from the viewpoints of family, vocation, church and community.) Encourage group discussion.

4. Ask: In what ways do you see that this group's knowledge of our spiritual gifts will benefit our church? Discuss.

5. **Five minutes before the one and one-half hour are up:** Stand up and invite the group to stand with you and join hands. Ask for sentence prayers of thanksgiving and blessing. Offer the concluding prayer and **dismiss on or before the scheduled time.** Your group will appreciate your considerate and faithful leadership.

Scriptural Identification of Spiritual Gifts

Week 2—Day 1

The Value of Knowing Your Spiritual Gifts

Your mind-opening sentence prayer for today's search:

1. A stimulating starter: Ephesians 4:12-16 (*The Living Bible*).

2. From these scriptures, list six reasons why God gives us unique spiritual gifts.

    1.

    2.

    3.

    4.

    5.

    6.

3. Listen to Ken Kinghorn's six ideas on why we should understand our spiritual gifts. They are on tape number three, "Discovering Your Spiritual Gifts." Stop the tape for today when you come to the section Ken calls "How Do I Discover My Spiritual Gifts?" Next, outline Ken's six ideas and compare them with the six you gleaned from the Bible.

    1.

    2.

    3.

    4.

    5.

    6.

Your insight from today's search:

Week 2—Day 2

How You Can Discover Your Spiritual Gifts

Your mind-opening sentence prayer for today's search:

---

1. Today, let Peter motivate you: 2 Peter 1:2-3; 5-6; 10 (*The Living Bible*).

2. What relationship do you see between the scripture you read and your search for your spiritual gifts? Write down two, three or four ideas.

3. Listen to the last part of the tape, "Discovering Your Spiritual Gifts." It starts with Ken asking: "How do I discover my spiritual gifts?" Write down his six ideas.

1.

2.

3.

4.

5.

6.

Your insight from today's search:

Week 2—Day 3

Identifying Seven Gifts

Your mind-opening sentence prayer for today's search:

---

1. Today's motivator: 2 Peter 1:10 (*The Living Bible*).

2. Thinking of your current quest, paraphrase this scripture verse, addressing it directly to yourself.

3. Read Romans 12:6-8 in several translations. These scriptures enumerate seven gifts. List them below. Next, in three or four words write the instructions regarding the use of each gift.

Gift	Instructions for Use
1.	
2.	
3.	
4.	
5.	
6.	
7.	

Your insight from today's search:

Week 2—Day 4

Identifying Eight More Spiritual Gifts

Your mind-opening sentence prayer for today's search:

---

1. Notice these beautiful spirit-charging verses: Philippians 4:6, 19.

2. As an exercise in reaffirming your faith, list some needs you would like to have God fill. As Paul reminds you in this passage, thank God. Then move on with your search.

3. Turn to 1 Corinthians 12:8-11. Use different translations. You will find nine spiritual gifts. One is a repeat of yesterday's discovery. List all nine gifts. Indicate with an asterisk (*) the repeat gift.

1.

2.

3.

4.

5.

6.

7.

8.

9.

Your insight from today's search:

Week 2—Day 5

Identifying Five More Spiritual Gifts

Your mind-opening sentence prayer for today's search:

---

1. A prize scripture for tuning in to the Lord: Psalm 103:1-2.

2. How does your inner being respond to today's tune-in scripture? Write two to four sentences.

3. Today you will search 1 Corinthians 12:28-30 and Ephesians 4:11. In them you will find five new spiritual gifts and six you have previously discovered. Again, indicate with an asterisk (*) the gifts repeated.

    1.   2.

    3.   4.

    5.   6.

    7.   8.

    9.   10.

11.

4. Over the past three days you should have dug 20 spiritual gifts out of the Bible. Check your list of the spiritual gifts with Ken's. Find his on page 10 of the booklet, *Discovering Your Spiritual Gifts.*

Your insight from today's search:

Week 2—Day 6

Spiritual Gifts and Your Relationships

Your mind-opening sentence prayer for today's search:

---

1. Get on the Lord's wavelength: Psalm 20:4-5.

2. For maximum impact, write down what the two verses say to you in two to four sentences.

3. Listen to the fourth tape, "Spiritual Gifts and The Church." The first third of the tape contains questions and answers. If you lack time today, listen to the first third of the tape tomorrow on catch-up day. Be relaxed and take time to capture Ken's interpretations of the powerful ways to use spiritual gifts in your local church and your relationships. Be on the lookout for five inspired ideas. Make them yours by writing them down and including as many subpoints as possible. If you have questions, take them to your Group Exploration and Celebration.

    1.

    2.

    3.

    4.

    5.

4. Before laying aside your study materials, write your "mind-opening sentence prayer."

Your insight from today's search:

Week 2

Group Exploration and Celebration

Your mind-opening sentence prayer for today's exploration and celebration:

Name of leader ___________________________________

A. Preparation directions for the leader:

1. Read addendum, pages 75-76, "Tips for Search Groups Leaders."

2. Make sure everyone has filled in "your mind-opening prayer." If not, take time for everyone to fill it in.

B. Bringing People's Hearts Together (30 minutes)

1. 20 minutes—Let informality and spontaneity be the atmosphere in which you bring your group together. First have every person share one good thing that has happened to him/her in the past week. Next let each person share personal news, joy and concerns, particularly centering on family, vocation, church and community. Include requests for prayer and prayers of thanksgiving for specific good things happening in the lives of group members.

2. 10 minutes—(a) Let each person read his/her mind-opening prayer for today's group experience with a prayerful attitude. (b) Stand in a circle to form a bond of fellowship with everyone holding hands. Ask each person to pray silently for the person on his/her right. Upon completion of each silent prayer, have every person squeeze the hand of the individual on his/her right. Next, repeat the process by asking all to pray silently for the person on their left. (c) Finally, open the floor for verbal sentence prayers from those who feel comfortable praying aloud. Suggest a special emphasis on praise for the ability to come together and petition for the presence and leading of the Holy Spirit. As the leader, you should conclude these brief prayers.

C. Answers and Affirmation (approximately 15 minutes)

In a relaxed fashion and in a spirit of full acceptance of each others' ideas, raise these thoughts for sharing and discussion:

1. As an opener let each person share **one idea only** from this week's study that was meaningful to him/her. Ask why it was meaningful.

2. Ask people if they have questions that came out of the past week's search. Give group members time to collect their thoughts. Let the group answer the questions. If the group is reluctant to respond, simply choose a specific individual and ask, "(Name), how would you answer that question?" If you and the person who raises the question are satisfied with the answer, go on. If not, let the group respond or ask someone else. Then cover any other questions the group might have. Keep the discussion moving and positive. When the number of questions slows down or runs out, go to the group exploration.

D. Group Exploration (10-12 minutes for each question)

1. Ask: Why can we expect our individual ministries to be more effective when we become confident of our spiritual gifts?

2. Ask: At this point most of us are speculating about our spiritual gifts. Let's share what we think our top two spiritual gifts might be. (Assure them that later they will be more positive of what their gifts are.) Take note of each person's name and his or her expected gifts.

3. Ask: As we come to know our spiritual gifts, what are some ways in which we can expect to accelerate the ministry of our church?

4. **Five minutes before the one and one-half hour period is up:** Stand up and invite the group to stand with you and join hands. Ask for sentence prayers of thanksgiving and blessing. Offer the concluding prayer and **dismiss on or before the scheduled time.** Your group will appreciate your considerate and faithful leadership.

Function of Each Spiritual Gift

Week 3—Day 1

Functions: Administration, Apostleship, Compassion and Discernment

---

Your mind-opening sentence prayer for today's search:

Introduction to week three: Now you will start digging deeper into the functions of the 20 different spiritual gifts. Giving yourself to God through a prayerful, thoughtful and searching attitude, you will examine the use of each gift and then relate it to your own experience. With patience, thoroughly examine the gifts. By keeping an open mind and letting the Holy Spirit be your guide and illuminator, your major gifts will emerge. Often this exercise becomes a life-changing and/or life-charging experience. Expect both. May God bless your search.

1. For maximizing your attitude to receive God's word today: Hebrews 13:21 (*Today's English Version*).

2. Write what the scripture says to you relative to your study in two or three sentences.

3. Look on page 11 of *Discovering Your Spiritual Gifts* and carefully study the functions of the first four gifts. They are administration, apostleship, compassion and discernment.

4. Write one or two specific examples of ways you have used each gift or seen it used. Recall examples from the recesses of your mind. Think hard, but if you cannot recall an example, write "none."

Gift

Examples from your life or from others' lives

Administration

Gift	Examples from your life or from others' lives
Apostleship	
Compassion	
Discernment	

Your insight from today's search:

Week 3—Day 2

Functions: Evangelism, Exhortation, Faith and Giving

Your mind-opening sentence prayer for today's search:

---

1. Your attitude conditioner: Philippians 4:19 (*Phillips*).

2. Write below the encouragement you received from the scripture as it pertains to your quest.

3. The four gifts for today's study are evangelism, exhortation, faith and giving (pages 11-12, *Discovering Your Spiritual Gifts*).

4. After carefully studying and absorbing the functions of these four gifts, as you did with yesterday's gift study, relate your experience to the gift.

Gift	Examples from your life or from others' lives

Evangelism

Gift   Examples from your life or from others' lives

Exhortation

Faith

Giving

Your insight from today's search:

Week 3—Day 3

Functions: Giving Aid, Healing, Helps and Miracles

Your mind-opening sentence prayer for today's search:

---

1. Putting your search in the Lord's hands: Exodus 33:13 (*The Living Bible*).

2. Pause, think and write how Moses' prayer applies to your exploration.

3. The four spiritual gifts you will study today are giving aid, healing, helps and miracles (page 12, *Discovering Your Spiritual Gifts*).

4. After studying these gifts, relate experiences from your life, preferably, or from the lives of others:

Gift	Examples from your life or from others' lives
Giving aid

Gift	Examples from your life or from others' lives

Healing

Helps

Miracles

Your insight from today's search:

Week 3—Day 4

Functions: Prophecy, Teaching, Tongues and Interpretation of Tongues

Your mind-opening prayer for today's search:

1. Sharpen your ability to search by letting God's Word sink deeply into your thinking: Numbers 14:8.

2. Write the thoughts about this verse that apply to your exploration to determine your spiritual gifts.

3. Today you examine the functions of the following spiritual gifts: prophecy, teaching, tongues and interpretion of tongues (pages 12-13, *Discovering Your Spiritual Gifts*).

4. In what ways do you relate to these spiritual gifts?

Gift

Examples from your life or from others' lives

Prophecy

Gift	Examples from your life or from others' lives
Teaching	
Tongues	
Interpretation of Tongues	

Your insight from today's search:

Week 3—Day 5

Functions: Serving, Shepherding, Word of Knowledge and Word of Wisdom

---

Your mind-opening sentence prayer for today's search:

---

1. For renewed confidence as you dig deeper: Psalm 37:5 (*King James Version*).

2. Try transplanting the meaning of this scripture to your life as you reach out to identify your four major spiritual gifts. Write your thoughts in two or three sentences.

3. The four gifts for investigation today are serving, shepherding, word of knowledge and word of wisdom (page 13, *Discovering Your Spiritual Gifts*).

4. To capture today's insights, continue to recall experiences you have had or have seen pertaining to these gifts. Give priority to your own experience.

Gift	Examples from your life or from others' lives
Serving	

Gift	Examples from your life or from others' lives
Shepherding	
Word of Knowledge	
Word of Wisdom	

Your insight from today's search:

Week 3—Day 6

Evaluation: Functions of Spiritual Gifts and Your Experience

Your mind-opening sentence prayer for today's search:

Today you will move closer to discovering your primary spiritual gifts. (Remember, some people may have two spiritual gifts. Others may find as many as six. We use four as a standard number.) You will begin to draw conclusions. Danger: Don't jump at your first conclusion. It may be the real thing, but consider the evidence and pray. Hold your insights in prayerful abeyance until next week when you will be better equipped to determine your gifts.

1. To move into this critical phase of your search for your spiritual gifts read: James 1:5-6 (*Revised Standard Version*).

2. Write two or three ideas of how these words from the Bible can help you make your great discovery.

3. Now take a little time to reflect on the functions of the different gifts. Then consider these self-analyzing thoughts. Which four spiritual gifts (a) are the most attractive to me, (b) make me feel most comfortable, (c) do I understand the best, (d) have I used the most, (e) relate particularly to the things I like to do? The experiences you wrote down pertaining to the spiritual gifts will help you respond.

4. Keeping an open mind and realizing this is your preliminary conclusion, list what you now consider your top four gifts.

1.________________________________   2.________________________________

3.________________________________   4.________________________________

5. Suppose the Lord stands before you and says, "Take whichever spiritual gift you want, no conditions attached." Which gift would you pick? It may or may not be one of the four you listed.
Your choice _______________________________.

6. To clarify your thinking, write **only one** sentence about each gift you listed, explaining why you think it is one of your four gifts.

1.

2.

3.

4.

7. Fill in your "mind-opening sentence prayer" on the next page. You will need it for your next group meeting.

____

Your insight from today's search:

____

Week 3

Group Exploration and Celebration

Your mind-opening sentence prayer for today's exploration and celebration:

Name of leader ________________________________

A. Preparation directions for the leader:

1. Read addendum, pages 75-76, "Tips for Search Group Leaders."

2. Make sure everyone has filled in "your mind-opening prayer." If not, take time for everyone to fill it in.

3. Before today's meeting the leader should have written every person's name on four pieces of paper and scrambled the pieces of paper in a box or basket. Before closing today, have every person draw four different names. (See point E, Group Assignment.)

B. Bringing People's Hearts Together (30 minutes)

1. 20 minutes—Let informality and spontaneity be the atmosphere in which you bring your group together. First have every person share one good thing that has happened to him/her in the past week. Next let each person share personal news, joy and concerns, particularly centering on family, vocation, church and community. Include requests for prayer and prayers of thanksgiving for specific good things happening in the lives of the group members.

2. 10 minutes—(a) Let each person read his/her mind-opening prayer for today's group experience with a prayerful attitude. (b) Stand in a circle to form a bond of fellowship with everyone holding hands. Ask each person to pray silently for the person on his/her right. Upon completion of each silent prayer, have every person squeeze the hand of the individual on his/her right. Next, repeat the process by asking all to pray silently for the person on their left. (c) **New for today:** Introduce "phrase praying." Encourage **everyone** to contribute a phrase of petition or praise. Possible phrases: "Thanks, Lord, for bringing us together," "Help me to discern my gifts," "Bless Jeanette and her mother." When everyone has shared a phrase, you, as the leader, should conclude the phrase prayers with a summary prayer for direction and blessing on the group's thinking.

C. Celebration, Answers and Affirmation (15 minutes)

In a relaxed fashion and in a spirit of full acceptance of each others' ideas, raise these thoughts for sharing and discussion.

1. As an opener, let each person quickly share his/her **most exciting idea** from this past week's exploration.

2. At this point, ask for questions that may have come out of this past week's search. Allow time for the members of your group to collect their thoughts. Let group members answer the questions that come up. If the group is reluctant to respond, simply choose a specific individual and ask, "(Name), how would you answer that question?" If you and the person who raises the question are satisfied with the answer, go on. If not, let the group respond or ask someone else. Then cover any other questions that the group might have. Keep the discussion moving and positive. When the number of questions slows down or runs out, go to the group exploration.

D. Group Exploration

1. Let's speculate (10 minutes):

a. Why do we draw a preliminary conclusion on our top four spiritual gifts?

b. Why do we consider gifts that may not be listed in the preliminary conclusion on our top four?

2. Let each person share (only 10 minutes total):
If you could pick only one gift, which would you choose? Why?

3. Share your preliminary conclusions (10 minutes total).

a. Have each person, without explaining why, share what he/she expects his/her top four gifts to be. The group should not comment at this time.

b. Have the rest of the group write down on the next sheet the four spiritual gifts each one expects to discover.

E. Group Assignment

1. The drawing: Each person should keep in thought and prayer the four different people whose names were drawn at random. If someone is absent have another person draw for the absentee and deliver the names to that person. Each person should place an asterisk on the next page by the four names they draw.

2. Be thinking about and be in prayer regarding the spiritual gifts you see in your fellow group members. This will be an exciting week.

F.   Five minutes before the one and one-half hour period is up: Stand up and invite the group to stand with you and join hands. Ask for sentence prayers of thanksgiving and blessing. Offer the concluding prayer and **dismiss on or before the scheduled time.** Your group will appreciate your considerate and faithful leadership.

Potential Spiritual Gifts of Group Members

1. Name _______________________

    a.

    b.

    c.

    d.

2. Name _______________________

    a.

    b.

    c.

    d.

3. Name _______________________

    a.

    b.

    c.

    d.

4. Name _______________________

    a.

    b.

    c.

    d.

5. Name _______________________

    a.

    b.

    c.

    d.

6. Name _______________________

    a.

    b.

    c.

    d.

7. Name _______________________

    a.

    b.

    c.

    d.

8. Name _______________________

    a.

    b.

    c.

    d.

9. Name _______________________

    a.

    b.

    c.

    d.

10. Name _______________________

    a.

    b.

    c.

    d.

11. Name _______________________

    a.

    b.

    c.

    d.

12. Name _______________________

    a.

    b.

    c.

    d.

Place an asterisk (*) by the names you drew out of the basket.

Discovering Your Spiritual Gifts

Week 4—Day 1

Considering Your Friends

Your mind-opening sentence prayer for today's search:

---

1. One of the great benefits of your group experience is the way you encourage, appraise and affirm each other. This often happens in subtle, unnoticed ways. However, we now come to a very positive and visible method of ministering to one another. A reminder of the importance of group concern: 1 Peter 4:8-11.

2. Write two ideas that will help you translate the scripture into group concern.

3. At this time, thinking of your group:

    a. List all the names of the people in your group on the next page.

    b. After listing the names, picture each person in your group. Then, based on your judgment, list two or more spiritual gifts you think each person might have. At this moment, do not refer to the spiritual gifts the people listed themselves. It is your perception that counts in answering this question.

    c. After completing the assessment of your friends' spiritual gifts, compare your ideas with theirs. Do not accept or reject any differences of opinion but think and pray about them. Keep in mind that some social scientists say that it is possible for a friend to understand another individual better than that individual understands himself/herself.

Your insight from today's search:

What you perceive the spiritual gifts of your friends in your search group to be (two gifts for each person, more if you can think of them):

1. Name_______________________

   a.
   b.
   c.
   d.

2. Name_______________________

   a.
   b.
   c.
   d.

3. Name_______________________

   a.
   b.
   c.
   d.

4. Name_______________________

   a.
   b.
   c.
   d.

5. Name_______________________

   a.
   b.
   c.
   d.

6. Name_______________________

   a.
   b.
   c.
   d.

7. Name_______________________

   a.
   b.
   c.
   d.

8. Name_______________________

   a.
   b.
   c.
   d.

9. Name_______________________

   a.
   b.
   c.
   d.

10. Name_______________________

   a.
   b.
   c.
   d.

11. Name_______________________

   a.
   b.
   c.
   d.

12. Name_______________________

   a.
   b.
   c.
   d.

Week 4—Day 2

Taking Inventory—First Day

Your mind-opening sentence prayer for today's search:

---

1. The moment of great discovery is close. Recalling the third Discipline for the Venture, page 3, "You may choose to speed up or slow down the schedule," and considering the excitement of the imminent discovery, this may be the time for lingering longer or finishing faster. Anchor your feelings in a prayer for understanding and insight.

2. Beginning your inventory: Psalm 51:6 (*The Living Bible*).

3. After a prayerful reading of this scripture, respond to the Lord by writing two or three sentences explaining the scriptural guidance you received from it as you start your inventory.

4. Carefully read page 14 in the booklet, *Discovering Your Spiritual Gifts.* Start your inventory, rating yourself on a scale of 0-5 on the first 100 statements beginning on page 15. The second 100 will be rated tomorrow, unless you decide to finish faster.

Your insight from today's search:

Week 4—Day 3

Taking Inventory—Second Day

Your mind-opening sentence prayer for today's search:

---

1. Search out one of the Bible's most popular portions of scripture in any translations you have: Proverbs 3:5-6.

2. In two or three sentences, apply the scripture to your inventory exercises today.

3. Beginning with statement 101 on page 20 of *Discovering Your Spiritual Gifts,* rate yourself 0-5, as you did yesterday, all the way through statement 200 on page 26.

4. Tomorrow is the big day. You add up the score. Pray that you will understand the results.

Your insight from today's search:

Week 4—Day 4

Taking Inventory—Third Day

Your mind-opening sentence prayer for today's search:

---

1. This is the day of your great discovery! Let God's Word prepare your heart, mind and attitude for letting this great discovery enrich and make your life effective beyond imagination: Romans 11:36, 12:3.

2. Write your understanding of the scriptures as they apply to the spiritual gifts you are about to discover. Again, limit your thoughts to two or three important but simple statements.

3. Discover your top spiritual gifts:

   a. List your ratings of statements 1-200 on the response sheet in the center of *Discovering Your Spiritual Gifts.*

   b. Add up each one of the 20 horizontal lines, A through T, putting the result of each line under "total."

   c. List the gifts at the end of each line, A through T. Your key is on page 28, *Discovering Your Spiritual Gifts.*

   d. Next list your four highest scores and the corresponding gifts on page 27.

4. Pause. Thank God for your gifts. Pray that you will understand how to use them as He wants you to.

Your insight from today's search:

Week 4—Day 5

Your Response—Your Spiritual Gifts

Your mind-opening sentence prayer for today's search:

---

1. Today's scripture: Romans 12:1-2 (*The Living Bible*).

2. What does this scripture say to you as you pause to reflect on your top four spiritual gifts? Condense your thoughts into 20 or 30 words and write them below.

3. Check the **one** idea that comes closest to your feelings about how your inventory came out.

( ) as expected   ( ) surprised   ( ) do not understand

( ) elated   ( ) confused   ( ) disappointed

4. To help clarify the results, and your own feelings, briefly describe why you answered question three as you did.

5. Now, think through this question: Going back to question three, does your first reaction to your inventoried gifts raise

( ) possibilities or   ( ) questions?

6. List those possibilities or questions.

1.

2.

3.

4.

7. Tips on discovering and relating to spiritual gifts:

1. Reviewing the definitions of spiritual gifts often helps clarify their meaning in an individual's life (pages 11-13 in *Discovering Your Spiritual Gifts*). A detailed treatment of spiritual gifts can be found in *Gifts of the Spirit,* by Ken Kinghorn (Abingdon Press).

2. Sometimes it takes prayer and a little time to relate your spiritual gifts to God's current plan for your life.

3. If you can see an immediate use for your gift(s), remember this is just the beginning. There is no way of knowing where God will lead.

4. Wait on the Lord for a clear revelation and direction for appropriating the supernatural power that can flow through your gifts.

5. Remember that the gifts are of God. Thank Him for them. As you open your heart and mind, giving yourself to God, the Holy Spirit will work through your spiritual gifts to do things you would never have imagined possible!

Sharing an experience: Barbara was confident that she had the gift of *evangelism.* It did not show up on her inventory. Thinking there was a mistake, she did the inventory three times. The results were the same. Her unexpected gift was *administration.* She prayed and pondered. One day her confusion cleared up. Using her administrative gifts, she had organized an *evangelism program* for her church. The evangelists in the church evangelized and the administrator put it all together and made it work. Everybody wins when we let the Lord use our gifts!

____

Your insight from today's search:

____

Week 4—Day 6

Thinking of Others

Your mind-opening sentence prayer for today's search:

---

1. Major benefits from this group search include supporting, encouraging, appraising and affirming each other. Devote today's 30 minutes to thinking and praying for friends with whom you are sharing this venture.

2. Prepare your heart and mind for this rewarding effort: Hebrews 13:16.

3. Write your interpretation of the scripture as you think of the four people for whom you have been praying all week.

4. Compare your ideas of these four people's spiritual gifts with their expectations of what their gifts are: (a) if your listing of their gifts (Week 4—Day 1) is the same as theirs, consider it an affirmation; (b) if yours is different from theirs (Week 3—Group Exploration and Celebration), give thought as to why; (c) if you feel your evaluation is important and can be helpful, share that difference and your reason for it. Remember, the final identification of gifts remains between the individual and God. Your insight could be an important help.

5. List the names of the four people you have been praying for and thinking about this week.

1. ____________________________

2. ____________________________

3. ____________________________

4. ____________________________

6. Using your understanding of their gifts, think of something special each one of these four people is doing or could be doing to use those gifts. List the item(s) under his/her name in six words or less. Does your impression relate to the spiritual gifts they are expecting to determine? Withhold judgment until your group meeting. This is "seed planting" for next week's exciting experience.

7. With Hebrews 13:16 in mind, think and pray about one or more loving, definite and positive ways in which you can encourage, appraise, affirm or help each one of your four people. Write the idea under each name on the previous page.

8. Remember to write "your mind-opening sentence prayer" for Group Exploration and Celebration.

____

Your insight from today's search:

____

Week 4

Group Exploration and Celebration

Your mind-opening sentence prayer for today's exploration and celebration:

Name of leader _______________________________

A. Preparation directions for the leader:

1. Read addendum, pages 75-76, "Tips for Search Group Leaders."

2. Make sure everyone has filled in "your mind-opening prayer." If not, take time for everyone to fill it in.

B. Bringing People's Hearts Together (30 minutes)

1. 20 minutes—Let informality and spontaneity be the atmosphere in which you bring your group together. First have every person share one good thing that has happened to him/her in the past week. Next let each person share personal news, joy and concerns, particularly centering on family, vocation, church and community. Include requests for prayer and prayers of thanksgiving for specific good things happening in the lives of members of the group.

2. 10 minutes—(a) Let each person read his/her mind-opening prayer for today's group experience with a prayerful attitude. (b) Stand in a circle to form a bond of fellowship with everyone holding hands. Ask each person to pray silently for the person on his/her right. Upon completion of each silent prayer, have every person squeeze the hand of the individual on his/her right. Next, repeat the process by asking all to pray silently for the person on their left. (c) Again for today: Use phrase praying. Encourage **everyone** to contribute a phrase of petition or praise. Possible phrases: "Thanks Lord for bringing us together," "Help me to discern and use my gifts," "Bless Jeanette and her mother." When all have shared a phrase, you as leader should conclude the phrase prayers with a summary prayer for direction and blessing of the group's thinking.

C. Celebration, Answers and Affirmation

In a relaxed fashion and a spirit full of acceptance of each other's ideas, raise these thoughts for sharing and discussion.

1. Start off by letting each person share what he/she now considers to be his/her top four spiritual gifts.

2. As individuals share, have the rest of the group turn to Week 4—Day 1, page 45 and compare their estimates with the individual's current assessment of his/her spiritual gifts. Suggest that the participants write down what the individuals report. **Do not discuss this yet.**

3. After everyone has reported, **randomly** (not in sequence around the circle) specify an individual. Ask the four people who have his/her name to share their thoughts and prayers (Week 4—Day 6) about the individual's gifts and the possibilities for using those gifts. In an **easy, loving, give-and-take spirit,** make sure there is dialogue between the participant and his/her evaluators. As the leader, keep the discussion moving so every individual has the benefit of the thoughts of four concerned friends. Since time is limited you should take only five minutes to evaluate/affirm each person.

Sample evaluation: "Joan, I notice that you always seem to know the appropriate thing to say when a person needs encouragement. Perhaps you have the gift of exhortation. You could use that gift to build up new believers in our congregation and to encourage that Sunday school teacher who's been having a tough time with the third-graders."

Sample evaluation: "George, it is so easy for you to strike up conversations with people about spiritual matters. I think you have the gift of evangelism. Maybe you could help the pastor call on those who visit our church and on newcomers in our community."

D. Conclusion

1. **As a rare exception, only if it is absolutely necessary,** you may go beyond your normal closing time to include evaluation and affirmation of each person. **If you must exceed the scheduled time,** tell the group about it five minutes before the normal closing time to give people who must leave the opportunity to do so. By watching, guiding and monitoring discussions and cutting discussion short when necessary, you should conclude on time.

2. When all people have been encouraged and affirmed, immediately stand up and invite the group to stand with you and join hands. Ask for sentence prayers of thanksgiving for loving Christian friends and for blessings upon them. Offer individuals the opportunity to pray as the Holy Spirit leads them to. Then offer the concluding prayer.

E. Parting Announcement:

The highlight of our search experience occurs this week.

Using Spiritual Gifts in Your Areas of Influence

Week 5—Preface

Use It—Don't Lose It

"Again, it will be like a man going on a journey, who called his servants and entrusted his property to them. To one he gave five talents of money [For the purpose of your study you could insert *spiritual gifts* where *talents* are used], to another two talents, and to another one talent....Then he went on his journey.

"After a long time the master of those servants returned and settled accounts with them. The man who had received the five talents...said, 'you entrusted me with five talents. See, I have gained five more.'

"His master replied, 'Well done, good and faithful servant...I will put you in charge of many things....'

"The man with the two talents...said, 'you entrusted me with two talents; see, I have gained two more.'

"His master replied...'I will put you in charge of many things....'

"Then the man who had received the one talent came...he said...'I was afraid and went out and hid your talent in the ground. See here is what belongs to you.'

"His master replied, 'You wicked, lazy servant....you should have put my money on deposit with the bankers, so that when I returned I would have received it back with interest.
" 'Take the talent from him and give it to the one who has the ten talents.' "

Key phrases from Matthew 25:14-28

Discovering your spiritual gifts and using them leads to new, higher and more exciting levels of responsibility. Knowing about your spiritual gifts and not using them is condemned by Christ. He points out that they will be lost through lack of use.

As you approach this week, pray that God will make clear to you how He wants you to use your individual gifts to His glory.

Keep two things in mind:

1. You will encounter difficulties and risks as you find places to invest your gifts. Fear of rejection or set-backs is no excuse for not using your gifts in Christ's service (Matthew 25:25-29).

2. According to the apostle Paul, you are expected to use your gifts for the building of His Church (1 Corinthians 14:12).

Week 5—Day 1

Your Areas of Influence

____

Your mind-opening sentence prayer for today's search:

____

1. For the record, list again the four spiritual gifts entrusted to you:

1.__________________________   2.__________________________

3.__________________________   4.__________________________

2. A frame of reference for your search for the proper use of your spiritual gifts: John 17:18-20, Matthew 28:18-20 (*The Living Bible*).

3. In no more than three sentences, summarize what the Holy Spirit says to you relating these Scriptures to the use of your spiritual gifts.

4. Someone has said that most of us operate in five basic areas of influence. Which ones come to mind? Number one might be a clue to trigger your thinking. To check your answers, take a peek at the daily topics for the rest of the week.

1.__________________________   2.__________________________

3.__________________________   4.__________________________

5.__________________________

5. In three or four words, record on the following chart how your spiritual gifts can make you more effective in your areas of influence.

<u>Areas of Influence</u>   **<u>Use of Spiritual Gifts</u>**

1.

2.

3.

4.

5.

Your insight from today's search:

<u>Areas of Influence</u>   **<u>Use of Spiritual Gifts</u>**

Week 5—Day 2

Your Family

Your mind-opening sentence prayer for today's search:

---

1. Four different vignettes of family life are reported in Joshua 24:15, Luke 2:43-45, Luke 2:46-50 and Luke 15:20. After reading these scriptures, describe in a word or two the principle of family living you see described in each.

  1. Joshua 24:15

  2. Luke 2:43-45

  3. Luke 2:46-50

  4. Luke 15:20

Only after listing what the Holy Spirit said to you through God's Word should you compare your answers with others listed on page 74 of the addendum. During this search, also compare your answers with your friends'. Do not erase your first answers.

2. Name your spiritual gifts (one or more) that will help you reinforce and strengthen the principles for building strong families.

3. Take time in prayer and write at least one sentence on **how** one or more of your gifts (name each one) will help you strengthen each of the family-building principles you listed above.

1.

2.

3.

4.

Your insight from today's search:

Week 5—Day 3

Your Vocation

Your mind-opening sentence prayer for today's search:

---

1. As a help to realize your importance in Christ's grand plan of salvation for the world and the part your occupation or job has in His plans, read: John 17:16-18.

2. What do you hear as you reread the scripture? Write it down in 20 words or less.

3. United Methodist Bishop Emerson Colaw brings into sharp focus how our in-the-world jobs are used for Christ's purposes:

> When both pastor and people of the church are deeply dedicated and work together in the building of Christ's kingdom, fantastic things happen. Committed lay people lead more people to Jesus Christ than preacher, evangelist, books or any other method. They can renew and rebuild local congregations by sharing and caring with friends and neighbors in a community. They can penetrate all corners of the world by using their talents, occupational and recreational environments to communicate their faith in God.
>
> *Forward,* Dec. 1982

4. Listed below are seven powerful portions of scripture, Jesus' own words, that give us direction for our occupations. They also tell us of the strategic value of vocations in God's economy. Read the verse from your *Living Bible* and then write *your* interpretation. (Please follow the sequence. It was deliberately chosen.)

John 17:15

John 17:18

John 17:16

John 17:17

John 17:20

Matthew 25:21

Matthew 25:29-30

5. Write a conclusion of not more than three sentences telling how you view your job in relation to Jesus' high priestly prayer (John 17:22-23) and His ideas on using gifts.

6. Your conclusion is full of risks and rewards. Think of ways in which your spiritual gifts will help you to successfully fulfill the grand, exciting plan God has for your life. Itemize each of your key gifts. Spell out how you can employ each one of your spiritual gifts to make your career a more powerful witness. Plan a strategy to use your gifts for multiplying the opportunities God has given you. All this is done to glorify Christ, as He prays in John 17:22-23.

Spiritual gift 1

Spiritual gift 2

Spiritual gift 3

Spiritual gift 4

____

Your insight from today's search:

____

Week 5—Day 4

The Church

Your mind-opening sentence prayer for today's search:

---

1. Today you will start with Christ's command: "Therefore go and make disciples..." (Matthew 28:19). Also read Matthew 16:18, Acts 20:28 and 1 Corinthians 12:7.

2. Considering these three sources of scripture, write your impression of God's priority and concern for His Church in three sentences.

3. Write two sentences that tell how God makes it possible for all believers, regardless of vocation, to participate in building His Church. Today's scripture gives us clues.

4. Turn to the partial list of things needed to build Christ's Church on the next page. Add other items as you think of them.

5. List your gift or gifts next to the areas where they can be used.

6. List what **you** judge to be the best four ideas to help your church. Make sure they are compatible with your gifts.

1.

2.

3.

4.

7. Pray daily for one week about shifting your priorities to one or more of the four ideas listed above.

Building His Church

Your Gift (s)

Idea:

Evangelism

(example)

1. Teach a Sunday school class.

2. Sing in the choir.

3. Be a youth group counselor or assist one.

4. Visit new members, first-time visitors, the sick, the lonely or shut-ins.

5. Help start a new Sunday school class.

6. Help start a prayer-study group.

7. Pick up children for Sunday school.

8. Get your church to sponsor people participating in a "Discover God's Call" weekend.*

9. Help form a children's choir.

10. Help start a Bible study group.

11. Help start a church men's group.

12. Help start a sharing group.

13. Develop a tape ministry for shut-ins.

14. Organize search group(s) on the study, "What's God Saying...To Me?"*

15. Lead or assist in some work area of the church.

16. Teach the lesson for a women's group meeting.

17. Volunteer to assist the church staff in telephoning, mailing and other services.

18. Lead a Boy Scout or Girl Scout troop.

19. Lead a mid-week children's Bible study.

20. Encourage your church to host a "Weekend for Winners."*

21. Help in the nursery so mothers can participate in the mission of the church.

22. Lead or develop a stewardship consciousness group in your church to determine how to use members' time, talent and treasures.

23. Lead a Sunday school teacher's training program.

24. Your idea(s):

*See Addendum

Your insight from today's search:

Week 5—Day 5

Your Community

Your mind-opening sentence prayer for today's search:

1. As it did to Moses, let this scripture change your life and give it dimensions of immortality: "I have seen the anguish of my people in Egypt and have heard their cries. I have come to deliver them. Come, I will send you to Egypt" (Acts 7:34, *The Living Bible*).

2. Let the Holy Spirit speak to you as you apply this call to yourself by filling in the blanks below:

"I have seen the anguish of my people in ————————————————
(your community)
and have heard their cries. I have come to deliver them. Come, I will send
you, ———————————————— , to ———————————————— .
(your name)   (your community)

3. Pray for insight as you consider: Is something in my community causing pain, demeaning life, destroying human values, imprisoning people with hopelessness or robbing them of freedom and self-esteem? List one or two of those things below.

1.

2.

4. List the spiritual gift(s) that would be needed to deal with the situation(s) you listed.

   a. Situation description:

   b. Spiritual gift(s) needed: (1)________________ , (2)________________ ,

     (3)________________ , (4)________________

   a. Situation description:

   b. Spiritual gift(s) needed: (1) ________________ , (2)________________ ,

     (3)________________ , (4)________________

5. List again your four top spiritual gifts. Do any of these coincide with any of the gifts listed under point 4? If so, which ones?

   1.

   2.

   3.

   4.

6. Is there a relationship between your spiritual gifts and the gifts required to help remedy the anguish in your community? Praying in faith can reveal your part in correcting or minimizing the destructive nature of the situation(s) you see. Review again the God-Moses dialogue: Exodus 3 (*The Living Bible*).

Some prayer questions might be: Is this a ministry that can be handled through my church? Am I the one to spearhead it? If not, who? If you are the person to do it, pray for guidance in discussing the situation with your pastor, a trusted church leader and others that the Lord brings to your attention.

____

Your insight from today's search:

____

Week 5—Day 6

Your Recreation

Your mind-opening sentence prayer for today's search:

Today few people face the pressures and tensions of living that Jesus did. Familiar words and phrases surrounding Christ's activities are multitudes, thousands, people pressing in on Him, officials trying to trap Him, being pushed into the lake, selection of the disciples and their training.

Despite the constant, nagging urgencies of crowds, despite the acclaim, criticism, sneers and rejection, Jesus' spirit—although severely tested—remained strong and vibrant. There was no sign of "burn out."

1. These scriptures tell about Christ's secret of rebounding from extreme pressure to great, new miraculous accomplishments: Mark 6:46 and Luke 6:12.

2. In both instances, note the pressures Christ faced before praying and what happened after He prayed. Look at the context of these verses and list the circumstances surrounding His prayer.

   a. Circumstances before praying:

Mark 6:46

Luke 6:12

   b. Circumstances after praying:

Mark 6:46

Luke 6:12

3. Now examine the word "recreation." Webster defines it as, "refreshment in body or mind, as after work...."

4. Itemize four recreational activities that re-create and re-fresh you while giving you additional strength, enlarged vision, increasingly harmonious relationships (with God and people), ability for greater accomplishment and relaxation. Very likely, several more than four could be listed, but this is a good starting point. List more if they come to mind.

1.

2.

3.

4.

5. Next comes a tremendous question with life-changing possibilities. You might want to breathe a prayer before writing one or more ideas. Name the recreational activity (activities) that will help you develop the potential of your spiritual gifts.

1.

2.

3.

4.

6. Remember to write your "mind-opening prayer" for Group Exploration and Celebration.

Your insight from today's search:

Week 5

Group Exploration and Celebration

Your mind-opening sentence prayer for today's exploration and celebration:

Name of Leader ____

A. Preparation directions for the leader:

1. Read addendum, pages 75-76, "Tips for Search Group Leaders."

2. Make sure everyone has filled in "your mind-opening prayer." If not, take time for everyone to fill it in.

B. Bringing People's Hearts Together (30 minutes)

1. 20 minutes—Let informality and spontaneity be the atmosphere in which you bring your group together. First have every person share one good thing that has happened to him/her in the past week. Next let each person share personal news, joy and concerns, particularly centering on family, vocation, church and community. Include requests for prayer concerns and prayers of thanksgiving for specific good things happening in the lives of the group members.

2. 10 minutes—(a) Let each person read his/her mind-opening prayer for today's group experience with a prayerful attitude. (b) Stand in a circle to form a bond of fellowship with everyone holding hands. Ask each person to pray silently for the person on his/her right. Upon completion of each silent prayer, have every person squeeze the hand of the individual on his/her right. Next, repeat the process by asking all to pray silently for the person on their left. (c) Again for today: Use phrase praying. Encourage **everyone** to contribute a phrase of petition or praise. Possible phrases: "Thanks Lord for bringing us together," "Help me to discern and use my gifts," "Bless Jeanette and her mother." When everyone has shared a phrase, conclude the phrase prayers with a summary prayer for direction and blessing on the group's thinking.

C. Celebration, Answers and Affirmation

In a relaxed fashion and a spirit of full acceptance of each other's ideas, raise these thoughts for sharing and discussion:

1. Start off by letting each person share what he/she considers to be his/her top four spiritual gifts.

2. Group discussion for last week's search:

   a. Let each person share as the Holy Spirit speaks. Ask them: What was the best idea you discovered this week?

   b. In which area of influence do you feel your spiritual gifts will be most helpful?

   c. Take time for two or three people to share how they are going to use recreation to increase their effectiveness in using their gifts. Be sure they include the specific areas of recreation in which they will be involved.

D. Your Take-off

This is the time for general sharing about how the Holy Spirit has spoken to you about making your life more effective through the use of your spiritual gifts. Some questions to guide the discussion:

   1. What is one specific thing you have heard the Holy Spirit say about how to make your life more effective through the use of your spiritual gifts?

   2. How are you going to start using your gifts more effectively and when will you begin?

   3. What would you, as a group, think of planning an evening of sharing with other spiritual gifts search groups in the community and with the pastor and ministerial staff of your church to discuss what has come out of the search and how it might benefit the church?

E. Conclusion

   1. **Rare exception, only if it is absolutely necessary:** Go beyond your normal closing time to include evaluation and affirmation of each person. If you must exceed the scheduled time, tell the group about it five minutes before regular closing time to give the people who must leave the opportunity to do so. By watching, guiding, monitoring and cutting discussions short when necessary, you should conclude on time.

   2. When all people have been encouraged and affirmed, immediately stand up and invite the group to stand with you and join hands. Ask for sentence prayers of thanksgiving for loving Christian friends and for blessings for them. Offer the individuals the opportunity to pray as the Holy Spirit leads them. Offer the concluding prayer.

   3. Conclude by praying the Lord's Prayer in unison. Sing "Blest be the Tie that Binds."

Answers for true/false questions on Week 1—Day 2

1. **False.** Love is a spiritual fruit. Reference: Taped lecture, "An Introduction to Spiritual Gifts." Galatians 5:22-23.

2. **True.** Lay people are called to ministry just as pastors are. Reference: Taped lecture, "Discovering Your Spiritual Gifts." 1 Corinthians 12:7, 11.

3. **True.** Reference: *Discovering Your Spiritual Gifts,* p. 8. 1 Peter 4:10, Romans 12:6-8, Ephesians 3:20.

4. **False.** Spiritual gifts are given to Christians as a divine tool for ministry. Reference: Taped lecture, "An Introduction to Spiritual Gifts."

5. **True.** Reference: *Discovering Your Spiritual Gifts,* p. 27.

6. **True.** A spiritual gift is a supernatural ability given by God to enable a Christian to serve. Reference: *Discovering Your Spiritual Gifts,* p. 27. 1 Peter 4:10.

7. **False.** Talents are forms of ministry through which spiritual gifts can flow and be enhanced. Reference: Taped lecture, "An Introduction to Spiritual Gifts."

8. **True.** God gives us spiritual gifts when we commit our lives to serve Him. Reference: Taped lecture, "An Introduction to Spiritual Gifts."

9. **False.** Music is a talent. Reference: answer 7.

10. **True.** Reference: *Discovering Your Spiritual Gifts,* pp. 8-9.

11. **False.** Patience is a fruit of the Spirit. Reference: Taped lecture, "An Introduction to Spiritual Gifts." Galatians 5:22-23.

12. **False.** Spiritual gifts are gifts of God given only to Christ-committed people whose hearts are right with God. Gifts cannot be acquired through human efforts. Reference: Acts 8:18-21.

13. **True.** Through prayer and use, spiritual gifts can be developed for more effectiveness. Reference: Taped lecture, "Discovering Your Spiritual Gifts."

Score (number wrong and corresponding grade):

0-2   **excellent**
3-4   **good**
5-6   **try again**

One person's answers for Week 5—Day 2

Joshua 24:15	Family commitment to God
Luke 2:43-45	Family accountability
Luke 2:46-50	Children need to feel free to exercise spiritual urgings and understanding.
Luke 15:20	Dependability of family love, no matter what

Tips For Search Group Leaders

If leading a small study group is new to you, the following principles of group leadership should be helpful. If you are an old hand at group leadership, these ideas may refresh your experience.

1. The size of your group should be six to twelve people. If there are more than 12, the impact of your study will be greatly increased by breaking up into groups not exceeding 12 members.

2. The place in which you meet should be friendly, cozy and relaxing. Meeting in homes is most popular. Changing homes for each meeting contributes to group interest and fellowship. The church fellowship hall is an alternative place for a friendly atmosphere. Otherwise, find a room in the church that can be rearranged to suit your needs.

3. Small search groups provide an excellent opportunity for reaching out to marginally involved church members and non-churched friends. Many people outside the church will often gladly meet in homes but not in church. Thus the neighborhood group frequently becomes a port of entry for outsiders to the church. Try it!

4. Seating should be arranged in a circle so all participants can see each other.

5. Time for starting and closing should be definite and should be followed. **Start and end on time.** An hour and a half seems to be the best time frame. Take roughly 20 minutes for sharing experiences and thoughts, bringing the group's thinking together and relaxing for group participation. Then, take 10 minutes for prayer focused on the needs of the group, community and church as well as for the purpose of the meeting. No one should feel under obligation to pray out loud. Sentence prayers are preferred. After feeling the comfort and support of the group, silent pray-ers often become verbal pray-ers.

This leaves one hour for discussion. If dialogue is lively at closing time, **close!** Closing on a note of excitement leaves anticipation for the next meeting. Your group will give you credit for being faithful to their planned schedule.

6. Light conversation during the first 20 minutes is a good starter for building bridges of understanding and appreciation. Being sensitive to the thoughts each person offers reveals our love and understanding. We will discover things we can do to support and encourage each other, even how to fill the deep needs of those in our own group.

7. Close sessions with a bond of fellowship where all participants stand up and hold hands (if group members feel comfortable with this). Give an opportunity for two or three people (more as the fellowship grows) to give sentence prayers, striking notes of thanksgiving and celebration.

8. Don't include refreshments during your regular weekly meetings. This usually becomes a burden and keeps people from joining the group.

9. Don't push the group too fast. Gently lead the discussion toward greater depth.

10. Have a lot of questions ready. Listen attentively to the answers. Let others ask questions.

11. **Your role as a leader is to stimulate discussion. Keep a check on yourself. Never use the group as a captive audience. Generally, you should not share. Your job is to lead.**

12. Don't ask questions that can be answered yes or no. Ask questions requiring thoughtful, positive answers. Example: Not, "Did you like the section on defining spiritual gifts?" Instead ask, "What did you like best in the section defining spiritual gifts?"

13. Accept each response seriously and with appreciation.

14. Be sensitive to what a person means as well as what he or she says.

15. Don't be afraid of silence. That is an excellent time for the Holy Spirit to speak to each person involved. In silence wait on the Lord to see what He has to say.

16. Keep the discussion positive. Avoid controversy. Emphasize thoughts that will improve quality of living, stronger faith, greater service, closer relationships with Jesus Christ.

17. Balance the discussion by encouraging the shy people and directing the discussion away from the talker who dominates the group.

18. Do not worry if you cannot cover all questions listed for each session. A good, in-depth discussion is more important than perfunctorily covering every listed question.

19. Let the questions in this guide be a starting point, the thought primers. As you stimulate ideas, push those which will expand your group's thinking.

20. Finally, as leader of this venture you will have a very challenging and rewarding experience. It could well be a stepping stone to leadership of other groups needed for church renewal today.

There's More . . .

You are part of something big. Most likely it's bigger than you anticipated. When you're trusting the Lord that can be expected. God says, "Put me to the test and you will see that I will open the windows of heaven and pour out on you all kinds of good things" (Malachi 3:10, *Today's English Version*).

You are completing the search, *Discovering and Using Your Spiritual Gifts.* This is Opportunity 5 of a new program, "Discover God's Call," which is bringing renewal to scores of churches. It is sponsored by the Foundation For Evangelism and being developed in consultation with the General Board of Discipleship of the United Methodist Church. To date there are five "opportunities" in the program, all growing out of requests from people and churches bent on experiencing the exciting, unfolding will of God for their lives where they are now.

The five opportunities are:

1. **"Discover God's Call"** is an experience of home search and weekend retreat for laity. It is the parent program.

2. **"Enlarge My Call"** is designed for people who have discovered their call ("Discoverers") and who want to move into greater dimensions of living. It is only for people who have been through the parent program.

3. **"Weekend for Winners"** is adapted from "Discover God's Call" to be used as a weekend spiritual renewal experience in the local church. It is led by a team of two to four trained coordinators.

4. **"What's God Saying To Me?"** is a six-week small group search venture largely based on the Bible and the book, *Called To Be A Layman*, by Gus Gustafson. It can be done in the local church, in homes or as a neighborhood study. The program explores ways God might call and how a person can hear Him.

5. **"Discovering and Using Your Spiritual Gifts"** is also a small group search experience for church and neighborhood lasting five weeks. The discussion and inquiry format is based on the Bible, Dr. Ken Kinghorn's booklet, *Discovering Your Spiritual Gifts,* and four of his taped lectures on spiritual gifts. The concluding week explores ways of applying a person's gifts for God's purposes.

To receive further information on these programs, please return the coupon on the next page.

The Foundation for Evangelism, Regional Office
P.O. Box 507, Griffin, GA 30224
Phone: (404)228-8770

Dear Friends:

Please send me information on: (check your interest)

1. ( ) Discover God's Call
2. ( ) Enlarge My Call
3. ( ) Weekend for Winners
4. ( ) What's God Saying...To Me?
5. ( ) Discovering and Using My Spiritual Gifts

Name   Phone (include area code)

Address   City   State   Zip

Church   Pastor's Name